Contents

This fifty first edition published 2000

ISBN 0 7110 2707 2

© Ian Allan Publishing Ltd 2000

Published by Ian Allan Publishing

an imprint of Ian Allan Publishing Ltd,
Terminal House, Shepperton, Surrey TW17 8AS.
Printed by Ian Allan Printing Ltd, Riverdene Business Park, Hersham, Surrey KT12 4RG.

Code: 0003/L2

Front cover: D-ABEK-Boeing 737 of Lufthansa. *Austin J. Brown / Aviation Picture Library*

All photographs by Alan J. Wright unless otherwise indicated.

CIVIL AIRCRAFT MARKINGS 2000

Alan J. Wright

D1143531

Ian Allan
PUBLISHING